TARAN
AS A

BARBARA REGER

Endorsed by the American Tarantula Society.

ATS

CONTENTS

Dedication, 2
Foreword, 3
Spiders on Earth, 4
Spider Anatomy, 7
The Selection and Handling of Tarantulas, 12
Dangers for Tarantulas and Their Keepers, 19
Dinners and Dwellings for Tarantulas, 23
Times of Great Danger–Molting, 29
Notes on Tarantulas in Nature, 37
Breeding Tarantulas, 43
Raising Young Tarantulas, 49
Benefits to Man, 53
Very Common Tarantula Questions, 55
Where to Find the People, Resources and Books to
    Answer the Questions, 59
English Names, Scientific Names, and Habitats for
    Some Common Tarantulas, 61
Suggested Reading, 63
Index, 64

Photos and illustrations by Jay Reger and Barbara Reger.

© 1995 by T.F.H. Publications, Inc.

Distributed in the UNITED STATES to the Pet Trade by T.F.H. Publications, Inc., One T.F.H. Plaza, Neptune City, NJ 07753; distributed in the UNITED STATES to the Bookstore and Library Trade by National Book Network, Inc. 4720 Boston Way, Lanham MD 20706; in CANADA to the Pet Trade by H & L Pet Supplies Inc., 27 Kingston Crescent, Kitchener, Ontario N2B 2T6; Rolf C. Hagen Ltd., 3225 Sartelon Street, Montreal 382 Quebec; in CANADA to the Book Trade by Vanwell Publishing Ltd., 1 Northrup Crescent, St. Catharines, Ontario L2M 6P5; in ENGLAND by T.F.H. Publications, PO Box 15, Waterlooville PO7 6BQ; in AUSTRALIA AND THE SOUTH PACIFIC by T.F.H. (Australia), Pty. Ltd., Box 149, Brookvale 2100 N.S.W., Australia; in NEW ZEALAND by Brooklands Aquarium Ltd. 5 McGiven Drive, New Plymouth, RD1 New Zealand; in Japan by T.F.H. Publications, Japan—Jiro Tsuda, 10-12-3 Ohjidai, Sakura, Chiba 285, Japan; in SOUTH AFRICA by Lopis (Pty) Ltd., P.O. Box 39127, Booysens, 2016, Johannesburg, South Africa. Published by T.F.H. Publications, Inc.
MANUFACTURED IN THE UNITED STATES OF AMERICA
BY T.F.H. PUBLICATIONS, INC.

Dedication

This book is dedicated to very special people. First and foremost, it is dedicated to my sons, Ben and John. They proved to be outstanding field assistants with our tarantula studies in the southwest. They continue to be supportive of my quest for knowledge and are my greatest source of pride.

This book would also not have been possible if it were not for the continued patience and support of my loving parents, John and Kate Haymond. Since eighth grade, they have supported my unusual hobby, although at times I'm sure this strange fascination of mine has caused them some stress and concern. They have always believed in me and encouraged my endeavors.

I must also include my husband Jay Reger, who not only helped to photograph and illustrate this book, but also has been a positive influence in my life. I will be eternally grateful for his kindness and support.

There are also gentlemen who have helped to give me information and encouragement. Mr. Clifford Jacobson gave me the encouragement in eighth grade with my Science Fair Project and continued to allow me to teach his biology classes about spiders. Dr. James Berry, a biology professor at Butler University, has also offered me advice and support since 1969. He continues to be my friend and fellow spider enthusiast. He also helped by previewing this book. Dr. Robert Gale Breene III from South Texas has been very supportive of my work in the past year. He edited several earlier versions of this book. Mr. Rick C. West, a research associate for the Royal British Columbia Museum, did final editing for this book. His depth of knowledge on tarantulas proved invaluable.

Besides those very special people, I am grateful to Tom Mason, Vincent Roth, and Steve Skinner for the extra time and materials they have supplied me in my studies.

Foreword

I became fascinated with spiders over 22 years ago upon entering an eighth grade Science Fair, where I tested the effects of caffeine on garden spiders. I decided to start collecting tarantulas not long after and presently own and study the behavior of over 500 tarantulas representing various species from around the world. I try to collect at least four individuals of each species with the hope of having enough observations to form valid hypotheses on the behavioral patterns prior to molting. I keep daily records of their activities and do not jump to conclusions; I wait until I have witnessed the behavior enough times.

This book is designed to answer commonly asked questions that owners have about their tarantulas. Many of the questions have come from my seminars and past experience. As a teacher, I often find many interested people who hunger for accurate information regarding tarantulas. I've given demonstrations and talks to all age groups, from preschoolers to adults, always trying to dispel the fears that many people have regarding tarantulas. These fascinating creatures can bring hours of enjoyment to anyone deciding to care for them as pets. I hope those interested in tarantulas find this book helpful.

Barbara with her two sons, Ben and John.

Spiders on Earth

Tarantulas are the largest of the spiders. With only 85 genera and an estimated 800 species, though, they are a small part of the many thousands of species of spiders in the world. Over 35,000 spider species have been described to date.

Spiders can be found everywhere, and they have been roaming the earth for over 300 million years. It is thought that anywhere from 70% to as little as 25% of the total number of species have so far been described.

There are two main groups of spiders. The first is the trappers, or web builders that wait in webs to snare insects. The hunters and ambushers, or wandering spiders, seek out prey on plants or on the ground, capturing insects with their powerful legs and chelicerae.

Spiders are members of the phylum Arthropoda. They are invertebrates with jointed legs and a protective external exoskeleton. They differ from insects in that they have two major body segments, four pairs of legs and a pair of chelicerae instead of mandibles. They are also capable of producing silk from glands located in the abdomen. They use the silk for building webs to capture prey, lining burrows, aerial ballooning activities and wrapping eggs.

A Mexican Blonde (*Aphonopelma chalcodes*) that was recently collected. Note the narrow abdomen. Most tarantulas in the wild do not have the plump abdomens that well-fed pets do.

Spiders are probably the most important predators of insects. They do not harm plants, but can rid them of harmful arthropods. Their venom is used to paralyze their prey and begin the digestion process, and except for a few genera, they are virtually harmless to man. The tarantula is falsely accused of being dangerous. If it does deliver a bite to a human, the reaction would be similar to that of a bee sting. Certain Central and South American species have been found to have a potent poison. However, they appear to lack the ability to deliver it, at least to humans.

Tarantulas live in most warm climates throughout the world. There are estimated to be about 40 species of tarantulas (family Theraphosidae) found in the United States. Most tarantulas have a fairly long life span. A few have lived nearly 30 years in captivity. Some arboreal or tree-dwelling species have a much shorter life span.

Tarantulas belong to the

This
common
Chilean
tarantula
has grown
to the size
of a penny
after two
years.

class Arachnida. There are 11 orders of arachnids, including spiders, ticks and mites, daddy long legs or harvestmen, whipscorpions, tailless whipscorpions, ricinulids, micro whipscorpions, short-tailed whipscorpions, pseudoscorpions, scorpions and solfugids or windscorpions.

Like all arachnids, tarantulas have an exoskeleton that is hardened in some places and pliable in others. It serves as an outer casing that contains their internal organs suspended in an open blood bath circulatory system. In order to grow, tarantulas must molt, or shed their skin. In its first two years, the young spider may shed its skin several times a year. When some species reach six to ten years of age, they will generally continue to molt once a year. The mature male, upon its final molting, emerges with its enlarged pedipalps and mating spurs evident. After becoming adult, the male will usually die within six to nine months. In some species, the female may reproduce for the next ten years or more. Of course, these numbers refer to most North American ground-dwelling species. Some arboreal tarantulas have a shorter life-span and mature much earlier, such as the South American Pink Toe, which can mature in 14 months; the females only live a few years more.

Spider Anatomy

An adult male of the *Pamphobetus* species.

The best way to learn the name of each part of the tarantula is to study the diagrams on the following pages. The tarantula's body consists of two main body parts. The cephalothorax, or the head, and thorax combined, is toward the front or anterior, and the abdomen is toward the back or posterior. The abdomen is joined to the cephalothorax by a narrow stalk-like structure called the pedicel.

The eight legs are all attached to the cephalothorax. Each leg has seven segments. At the end of each leg are tiny claws that enable them to cling to surfaces as they climb.

There are two other pairs of appendages on the cephalothorax besides the legs. The first are the pedipalps, located in front of the legs. Tarantulas use them to help grab their prey. They are also used to move an egg sac or maneuver other objects. Upon molting, the adult male has developed palpal bulbs or emboli used in mating. Male spiders are unique in that they have developed secondary sexual organs. Dragonflies and damselflies are the only other animals to have secondary sexual organs, but theirs is simply a storage-basket type arrangement on the underside of the second segment on the abdomen.

After molting, the adult male spider builds a sperm web and secretes a drop of sperm from his abdomen on this special web. He then transfers it to his pedipalps by dabbing the emboli into the droplet of sperm, where it is stored until needed for transfer into the female's abdominal genital opening. The female is capable of storing this sperm in the spermatheca until she is prepared to fertilize and lay her eggs. If the female molts before she produces eggs, the spermatheca and retained sperm will be shed in the molting process.

The remaining appendages are the chelicerae, which contain the poison glands. These are

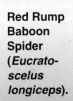

Red Rump
Baboon
Spider
(*Eucrato-*
scelus
longiceps).

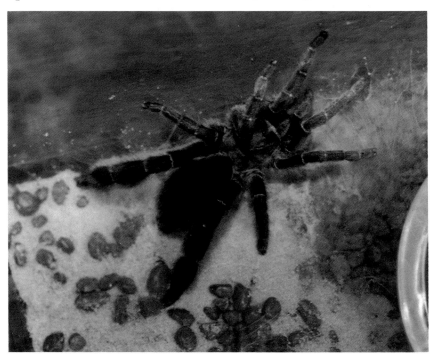

clawlike jaws to which the fangs are connected on the ends. These powerful appendages are used to dig a tarantula's burrow. Most spiders have horizontally moving fangs, but the Theraphosidae have vertically moving fangs.

The tarantula's eight eyes are visible in a small turret on top just behind the chelicerae. The hardened shield or shell where the eyes and foveal groove are located is often called the carapace. Also located within the cephalothorax are the sucking stomach and the brain.

The tarantula's body is covered with very sensitive hairs. Most tarantulas are thickly covered with hair on the abdomen. It is from here that tarantulas often throw urticating hairs at its enemies. These hairs are spiral barbs and are designed to irritate the eyes and nasal passages of attacking small vertebrate predators.

At the end of the abdomen are the spinnerets. The two pairs of fingerlike organs produce silk used for different purposes for the spider. Although most tarantulas, except the

arboreal kinds, do not spin webs to sit in, they use it for many other purposes. They lay upon a silken bed in order to molt, they may wrap up prey when it poses a threat, they line their

Below: A female Cobalt Blue (*Haplopelma lividus*).

burrows with it, and they wrap their eggs with it. Unlike in most spiders, the long pairs of spinnerets have muscles in them enabling them to manipulate the silk directly instead of moving the abdomen around, as in most other more advanced spiders.

The abdomen also contains the heart and the reproductive organs. On the underside, or ventral surface, of the abdomen, the genital opening is evident and the four book lungs are visible within the smooth areas. Wastes are excreted from the anus located near the spinnerets.

There is much speculation concerning the other senses of the tarantula. The hairs that cover their body are very sensitive to touch. Each contains nerves that send messages to the brain. It is known that the male spider can follow pheromones sent from the female to locate her for mating. I followed one male tarantula for over two miles in his search for a mate. Although no ears as such have been discovered, there is evidence that some spiders can detect sound or vibrations. The hypothesis is based on the fact that certain species are capable of producing sound.

The Mexican Blonde is abundant in the southwestern United States, especially throughout Arizona and New Mexico.

TARANTULA
VENTRAL VIEW

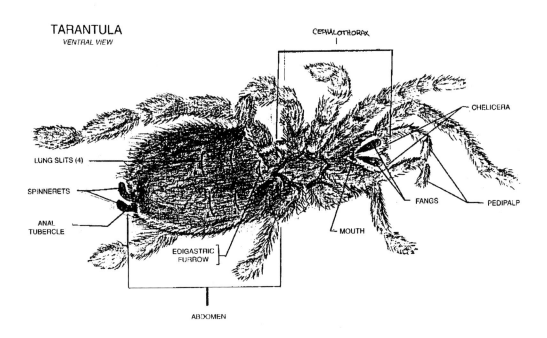

CEPHALOTHORAX

CHELICERA

LUNG SLITS (4)

SPINNERETS

ANAL TUBERCLE

FANGS

PEDIPALP

MOUTH

EDIGASTRIC FURROW

ABDOMEN

TARANTULA
DORSAL VIEW

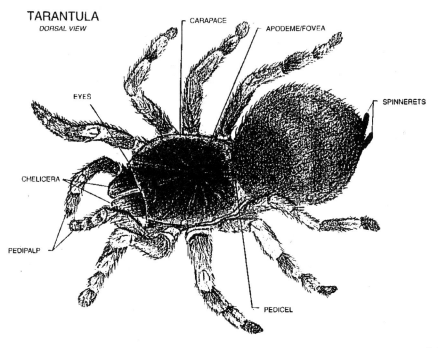

CARAPACE

APODEME/FOVEA

EYES

SPINNERETS

CHELICERA

PEDIPALP

PEDICEL

Illustrations:
by Jay Reger

The Selection and Handling of Tarantulas

The Thailand Black (*Haplopelma minax*) is an aggressive species that will readily bite.

Several books sold in pet stores contain helpful information on tarantulas. The authors often recommend some of their own favorite tarantulas for pets. Although I've used these books for years to make my selections, I have found, through observation of hundreds of tarantulas and in discussions with arachnologists and other tarantula owners, a certain amount of disagreement with some of the information presented. I have kept over a dozen different species in my school classroom at one time or another and have accumulated a fairly good body of knowledge about which species have proven the most gentle and reliable as pets.

To get an understanding of which tarantula species are the more aggressive ones, it is important to examine their defense mechanisms. For the most part, tarantulas with very hairy abdomens tend to prefer throwing hairs over biting. If you see a tarantula in a pet store that has a smooth abdomen with little hair, it will probably be inclined to use its fangs as a means of protection.

When threatened, these tarantulas will rear up on their hind legs with the front legs held high and fangs open. They will usually tap the offending intruder with their front legs several times as a warning before an actual strike. The Thailand Black, Cobalt Blue, Baboon Spider and most, if not all, of the other Old World tarantulas fall into this category. If you desire a pet that can occasionally be removed from its container to handle, then these species are not recommended.

Tarantulas with hairy abdomens also show aggression periodically by

When threatened, some tarantulas will raise their front legs, warning the intruder to leave them alone. This Thailand Black displays the typical threatening pose.

Mexican Red Leg (*Brachypelma emilia*).

rearing back and displaying their fangs, especially when they are newly captured and unaccustomed to their surroundings. If you use a pencil or similar object to probe around near the tarantula while it is still in its container, you may be able to see its reaction and hence get a preview of its potential behavior. However, I have purchased several that initially displayed this attack position, but soon became gentle and allowed me to handle them. They may often do this when first collected from the wild, so it may not be surprising that captive-bred species tend not to act in this manner. After several years, however, the species having little hair on its abdomen may continue to be aggressive and difficult or impossible to handle.

It is often very difficult to obtain information about a particular tarantula purchased from a pet store. The store owners may not have been told which country the spiders came from and often use a bewildering number of common trade names to identify them, many of which are misleading. Unless they are captive bred, you may never know the true identity and native home of your tarantula. Some species can be described and illustrated through pictures, and this can help you search for an appropriate personal pet.

My favorite species is the Mexican Red Leg. They cannot be found in pet stores at present because they are thought to be endangered and have been placed on the Threatened Species List. However, Mexican Red Legs can be purchased from tarantula dealers trading in captive-bred stock.

I believe that virtually any tarantula that is commonly found in the United States

can make a very good pet. None of the American species that I own has ever tried to bite me. Often found in pet stores are the Texas Brown and the Mexican Blonde, both being common in parts of the United States.

One of the most gentle species going is the South American Pink Toe Tarantula. I let my students handle this species quite often. It is best to coax the Pink Toe gently onto your hand and allow it to walk from one hand to the next, since it is too quick and fragile to hold at the cephalothorax as is done with most of the other tarantulas. Because it normally lives in trees (arboreal), the likelihood that it will fall and be injured is kept to a minimum. I try to discourage people from letting any tarantula walk on them, since a fall could easily prove fatal to the spider. The tarantula has claws on its feet that allow it to cling to skin or fabric with great strength, but its body is heavy and the membrane on its abdomen soft; it will tear easily on impact, causing a speedy death from fluid loss. Pink Toe Tarantulas have special pads on their feet that allow the additional clinging power needed to grip onto surfaces. This tarantula matures

Young Pink Toe tarantulas' (*Avicularia avicularia*) coloring is in contrast to their adult patterns. As spiderlings, their toes are black and their legs are pink. As adults, they will have pink toes and black legs and bodies.

within 14–16 months (unlike the Texas Brown, which may take 10 to 12 years) and is colored a deep bluish black with pink at the end of each leg (at the feet or tarsal segments).

Pink Toe Tarantulas are easy to maintain, but they do require high humidity and an ample supply of water. I usually place a clean branch or other climbing structure in each tank. They often construct a small webbed enclosure or retreat, and will remain inside most of the time. Water can be sprayed on the retreat and the food placed in its opening. Pink Toes molt in their silken retreats and push their old skins from the web afterwards,

which drop to the ground or are incorporated into the wall of their silken retreat.

Another popular favorite is the Zebra or Striped Knee Tarantula. Pet stores often give this tarantula any one of several different trade names, so use the photographs to help you identify them. Although pictures cannot provide absolute certainty that you are getting a particular species, they can guide you in your selection.

The Costa Rican Zebra is a most personable species. Often mine will move its water dish around if it finds it empty. It has never attempted to bite me.

The Chile Rose Hair and the Haitian Brown are also

Costa Rican Zebra (*Aphonopelma seemanni*).

commonly encountered in pet stores. These species generally make pleasant pets, but some individuals can be somewhat aggressive. The only tarantula that has ever bitten me was a Haitian Brown. The bite raised only tiny bumps the size of mosquito bites on the skin and itched a bit. The urticating hairs some tarantulas kick or flick from their abdomen, using their back legs, have proven more irritating to me than the actual bite of a tarantula.

After choosing the species of tarantula you want, you need to pay attention to its appearance. A bald spot on its abdomen is normal and does not indicate poor health since the hairs will be replaced when it molts. If the store owners have been feeding the tarantula with crickets, and you see tiny brown balls in its cage, then you know it has been eating them. Unlike many spiders which leave their prey seemingly intact after sucking out the juices, tarantulas rend and macerate their prey as they remove the fluids. The end result of feeding on a cricket is a small dehydrated ball left in the cage, a positive health sign for the tarantula. On the other hand, if you see several live crickets, some of which may actually be crawling on the tarantula, and no sign that it has eaten any, don't buy it. Tarantulas stop eating prior to a molt, but unless you know for sure that this tarantula is preparing to molt, its lack of appetite may indicate illness.

If the tarantula moves readily when the cage is shifted, this can be another positive sign of good health. If you are courageous, try to pick the tarantula up and look underneath it for any signs of injury. To pick it up correctly, gently place your middle finger and thumb between its second and third pair of legs and lift.

Remember, it is not a good idea to let it crawl on you. If you want it to walk, place it in a larger container, but keep in mind tarantulas can move very rapidly when disturbed.

This Pink Toe is constructing an elaborate webbed entrance to her tree bark home prior to constructing her egg sac. A water dish is kept elevated near the entrance to her home to maintain high humidity levels for this species found in the rain forests of South America.

Dangers for Tarantulas and Their Keepers

Tarantulas can use their back legs to throw urticating hairs at an attacking enemy. These hairs are designed to get in the eyes and skin of the potential predator, and while the intruder is rubbing its eyes, the tarantula presumably can make its escape. The hair of some tarantula species can cause a much greater reaction to skin than others. Mexican Red Leg Tarantulas have caused me more skin irritation than any other species. They cause my hands to itch and occasionally raise little white bumps. It helps to clean their cages while wearing rubber gloves since the hairs remain in the tank and water dish. They seldom throw any hairs at me, hopefully because they are quite accustomed to my hand being in their cage.

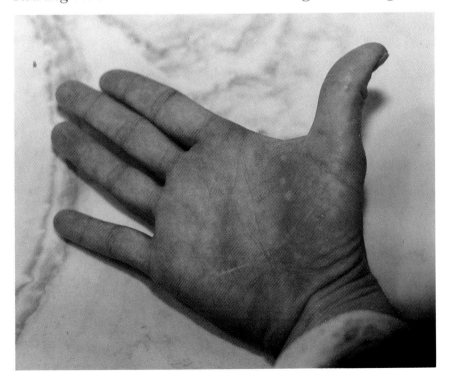

Urticating hairs from the abdomens of some tarantulas can cause itching and irritation to the skin of some people. The hairs caused the author's hand to become red and swollen with white bumps indicating where the hairs were embedded. This reaction occurred on the author after prolonged handling of a shed skin.

If you are bitten by a tarantula, it will feel like two bees stung you at the same time. The size of the tarantula's fangs, and the more aggressive the individual is, will determine how much the bite will hurt.

Many people fear that a bite from a tarantula will result in sickness or death. Unless a person has an allergic reaction to the bite, they will not die from it. Tarantulas do possess venom and the strength of the reaction will vary with the species of tarantula that has done the biting, but usually it will only cause much the same reaction as a bee sting. Just as some bee stings hurt more than others, tarantula bites also vary in their forcefulness. Some African Baboon Spiders and the South American Goliath Tarantulas have a vicious bite. It is not unusual for swelling and numbness to occur in the area of the puncture. The chances are greater for a person to react more unfavorably to the hairs of the abdomen than from the bite of most tarantulas.

Tarantulas have their own natural enemies just like most animals do. Besides man, their worst enemy is a spider-hunting wasp, of which the most common is the Pepsis wasp. In the wild, this wasp hunts tarantulas and paralyzes one with its sting before dragging it into a hole and laying an egg on it. The wasp larvae feed on the paralyzed tarantula, which keeps the larvae supplied with fresh food until near the time that it pupates. Some tarantulas found paralyzed have been rescued and have recovered from the paralyzing sting. Other tarantula enemies include small vertebrates (mice, rats, coatimundi, armadillos) and birds like road runners, hornbills and storks.

I'd like to caution tarantula owners against the use of insecticides around their tarantulas. Although several books warned me about insecticides, I felt enough precautions against it had been taken. When my dog brought fleas into my home, I decided to set off flea foggers. I removed all the tarantulas and placed them on my patio for a week. Before reintroducing them into my home, I washed down the walls and

shelves. My veterinarian said the spiders would be safe because the spray remained only in the carpet. I found out the hard way that it was also airborne. Within a week, I lost my two smallest spiderlings.

I removed all the spiders from my home, but the next three tarantulas to molt did not survive. It appeared that their new exoskeletons did not successfully harden. I used shampoo on the carpet and waited two more weeks before I brought my tarantulas home. These types of sprays can have a lasting lethal effect on your pet tarantula.

Mite infestations can also kill your tarantula. These little creatures are hard to spot on your pet. The best way to remove the mites is to pick off the external ones by hand. Sometimes putting a small amount of Vaseline on a Q-Tip and dabbing them off is very effective, as Al David mentions in his book *A Complete Introduction to Tarantulas*. Make sure the Vaseline does not get near their booklung slits or their mouth. Try to wipe it all off when finished. The introduction of predacious mites in the infected tarantula cage so they can prey upon the mite pests, leaving the spider alone, has also sometimes worked.

There are also certain Bot flies that parasitize tarantulas occasionally.

A life-threatening situation can occur if a tarantula is dropped, injured during a molt, or hurt in an encounter with another animal. The abdominal skin on the tarantula tears easily and the loss of hemolymph can occur rapidly. When I have gotten to them in time, I have saved several tarantulas by applying an alum mixture to the injury. I create this paste by mixing the powder with a small amount of water. This helps clotting to occur and the flow of hemolymph to stop. Al David suggests the use of dental cement on an injury. If the tarantula has sustained a very large wound, the chances are that nothing will save it. It will slowly die as the hemolymph flows from its body. This fluid is thick and transparent with a bluish tinge.

Man is an enemy of the tarantula. Most people fear these intriguing creatures and do not hesitate to destroy them. Large numbers of tarantulas are also lost crossing busy highways during mating season or after torrential rains have washed many from their burrows. Tarantula hunters looking for profit may strip entire areas of a species in order to sell them. One way to reduce indiscriminate collecting of tarantulas is to buy and sell only captive-born spiders to the pet trade.

Dinners and Dwellings for Tarantulas

Tarantulas require a minimum of maintenance. They are very inexpensive to feed and sustain. Your greatest expense will be for the tarantula itself, along with its cage and gravel. I use aquariums for my larger species and smaller enclosures for most other species. Spiderlings are best housed in small plastic containers because they readily maintain higher humidity. The tank itself need only be large enough for the tarantula to turn over when it is preparing to molt. If the base is at least twice as wide as the tarantula and twice as long, it will suffice. The height should not be taller than twice its leg span, since tarantulas do climb occasionally and falling on a sharp object could tear the thin membrane on its abdomen which may injure or kill it. If you own a burrow-dwelling species, then something should be placed in the cage so they can at least partially hide under it. Allow enough open space in the cage for them to molt. Arboreal tarantulas should have something to climb.

A variety of objects can be used to create artificial burrows. Sometimes, a young tarantula will dig its

This Mombassa Golden Starburst (*Pterinochilus murinus*) has just captured a cricket.

A Trinidad Chevron is seen devouring a cricket.

bottom to a small plastic container, all buried beneath the surface. They readily occupy this kind of housing and it allows them to feed naturally on insects that pass by the opening of the burrow.

Vermiculite is the preferable material for a substrate and has been successful for hundreds of tarantula tanks over the last eight years. I have found that soil may cause mold buildup or have an unpleasant odor. If you prefer to use soil, then make sure it is baked in the oven first to reduce the risk of mites or pathogens being present in the soil. In tanks where I needed to maintain moisture, I have sometimes used pine bark chips to help control the humidity. If your tarantula needs high humidity, you can always mist the tank with an atomizer on a regular basis. Placing a covering over most of the open slits or holes in the tank will also help to maintain a higher humidity. Species that live in rain forests need high humidity, and I will often lightly mist their tanks or keep two shallow dishes of water permanently present.

own burrow, but usually once it is grown, it occupies an available rock or hole. My favorite method is to break a small clay pot in half and turn it over in the tank. Paper towel cardboard tubes buried to the top can also be used. More elaborate tarantula habitats include deep tanks three–fourths filled with dirt, with hamster tubing attached at the

Some tarantulas can survive for long periods of time without food and water, but this should not happen in captivity. All your pets should have a constant supply if you want them to remain healthy. I use a shallow dish for most of my tarantulas. A glass dish that will not tip, such as an ashtray, is perfect for the spider. Small petri dishes are also fine for large tarantulas; they can straddle the bowl and lower their cephalothorax to drink from the dish. I have seen my large tarantula specimens doing this quite frequently. The water also will evaporate into the tank, supplying them with higher humidity.

Tarantulas will not overeat. They may get quite fat on what you give them, but they will not make themselves sick by eating too much. I feed my

A Goliath Bird Eater (*Theraphosa blondi*) with a small white mouse it has just killed.

A Trinidad Chevron devouring a pinky mouse.

tarantulas once a week with about two or three crickets each. This maintains a plump abdomen and keeps them satisfied. Crickets are a cheap source of food and can usually be purchased from a pet store or fishing bait shop. I strongly recommend varying their diet from time to time. In the spring, you can catch beetles, especially June beetles, moths, grasshoppers or insect larvae like caterpillars or beetle grubs to feed them. The June beetles are readily eaten by most tarantulas.

Since beetles represent about 40% of all insects (over 300,000 species), it makes sense that at least a part of their diet would be beetles. Some beetles are predacious or have sharp hooks or spines on their legs that are very strong. Avoid these because of possible harm to your pet. Large meal worms or small mice, frogs or lizards can be used for food as well. My Indian Ornamental Tarantula frequently eats lizards. Crickets are fine most of the time, but it is not wise to use them exclusively.

If you offer your tarantula prey and it does not appear interested in eating, then remove the insect from the container. Try to feed it again the next day. If it moves away from the insect or throws hairs at it, then it is best to remove the insect again. Tarantulas have reasons for not eating, such as they may be approaching a molt or are simply not hungry. Don't panic if your pet shows no signs of an appetite. Sometimes tarantulas will not eat for a few months. In nature, many species may stay in their burrows in the ground during winter and do not feed. Arboreal tarantulas usually feed year-round unless they are ready to molt. Regardless of the reason the tarantula is refusing the food, do not leave the insect in the cage for very long. The crickets tend to pick at the tarantula or annoy it and they can harm your pet. If the cricket

Here a Goliath Bird Eater is making a meal of a mouse.

annoys them enough, some tarantulas will eventually just kill the insect and not eat it. Others may be beginning the molt and cannot destroy it and, if so, this could cost your pet its life.

When you feed your pet on a regular basis, you will begin to become more familiar with its habits and start to know its basic needs. I feed mine on the same day each week and write down how much each one eats. This allows me to recognize changes in its behavior and become aware of signs of an upcoming molt.

One final consideration is the temperature. Most tarantulas will need a temperature of about 70 to 75 degrees Fahrenheit (22 to 26 degrees Celsius). Often people are advised to use a light bulb or heat lamp in the cage, but this could cause the tarantula harm should it get too close. If you cannot maintain this temperature in the room, then I suggest using a heated or "sizzle" stone (a small rock that provides a constant low heat for your spider). This stone is sold in most pet stores at a modest cost. My tarantulas will sit on them when they want the warmth and move off when they do not. It has never caused them harm and is a far superior method for the tarantula to regulate its body temperature. It senses when it's cold much better than we would. Sometimes, tarantulas will raise their body far from the ground when the gravel gets too cold or hot. You may even see them standing on the tips of their legs. Pay attention to unusual signs of behavior. You also may find them sitting on their water dishes frequently, and this may be a sign that the tarantula has greater humidity requirements. When you examine your pet on a daily basis, you can become familiar with its behavior and know when something needs to be done for its health or comfort.

Times of Great Danger— Molting

Tarantulas, as in all spiders, must shed their exoskeleton in order to grow and maintain their physiological systems. Female tarantulas carry on molting every year after becoming adult, but do not necessarily continue to grow. The first two years after hatching from eggs, they may shed several times. For the next two years after that, your pet may molt three or four times. Once they are around five or six years of age, they usually begin their annual molting routine and will molt at about the same time each year. Tarantulas in the United States and Mexico generally shed their skins in spring. Prior to the molting, large-scale complex internal changes happen inside the tarantula.

Most tarantulas will stop eating for two to three weeks before they shed their skin. They require a lot of water at this time and you may have to refill their water dish every other day. A few days before the molt, their

exposed abdominal skin will darken. The best indication of this is to observe any bald spot on their abdomen. Most of these places are orangish or light brown and they will turn black prior to a molt. Tarantulas should not be handled at this time since they are extremely soft and delicate and may die if moved.

Another activity at this time includes web bed

Shortly after molting, the white translucent fangs and greenish irridescent colors are visible in the Pink Toe. As the fangs harden, they will turn black.

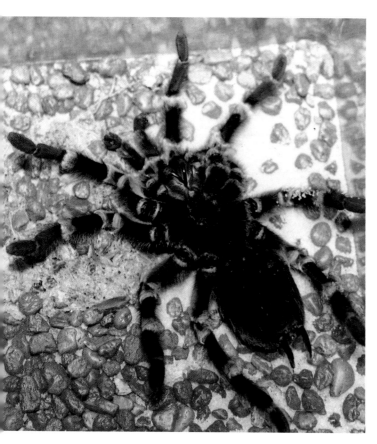

Most tarantulas turn onto their backs in order to molt, others lean on their sides, and a very few do it when they are right side up. The light weight of their exoskeleton helps them to push it up and off their legs, since most of the old exoskeleton has been re-digested for use in the new one.

I have noticed several different patterns of molting in the many different species. The arboreal species take less time in the molting process, while the Mexican

Above: A tarantula will turn onto its back or side as it prepares to molt. It may lie motionless for several hours before it emerges from its old skin.

construction. The tarantula will lay down a thin layer of silk to rest on while on its back waiting for its exoskeleton to detach. Al David mentions in his 1987 book that spiders in captivity will soon stop laying down a molting web bed. After many years and 500 tarantulas, all of mine have continued the behavior. The bed gets thicker over the years, but they continue to add to it.

Red Legs may stop eating for more than two months prior to a molt. However, these are exceptions. The average tarantula stops eating three weeks prior to the molt and it will begin drinking lots of water. One to two weeks before the molt, the abdomen, if bare, turns very dark and the day before the spider sheds, it begins to lay down a silken bed. On the day of the molt, it will turn on its back and lie motionless several hours before any movement can be seen; then the skin visibly begins to separate. Once the skin separates, the carapace will be exposed first. Some people call this initial step a "popping the top." Next, the abdomen is uncovered. The legs are the last part that the tarantula pulls free. The tarantula will rest between the pushing and again after the old exoskeleton or exuviae is free from its body. It may not turn right side up for another hour or so.

For the next two days, you may see your tarantula extending its legs way out. From the time the old exoskeleton comes off until the new one hardens, the tarantula will do its growing by means of hemolymph pressure expanding the legs and body. Its fangs will appear a translucent white for a couple of days. It cannot take any food until these have hardened and darkened again. Provide only water at this time and do not offer it any food. You will notice a much brighter and more colorful pet once the molting is complete. After a couple of days, offer your pet a cricket and if it is ready, it will snatch the prey. It will be quite hungry after its molting ordeal. If it shows no signs of wanting the insect, remove it immediately and try again in another two days.

If your tarantula is missing a leg or palp, it will be replaced generally during the next molt. The new limb will not be as large or colorful since it may take two or more molts to completely gain back its original stature. Males molt a final time into full adulthood; they are then capable of mating. Mating spurs on the front legs and enlarged pedipalps with bulbs or emboli, used to store sperm for mating, form under the old exoskeleton prior to the last molt. They rarely go through another

As a molt is imminent, the skin will darken. Here, a bald spot on the abdomen shows the blackish color of the skin.

This recently molted adult male Mexican Blonde is quite different in appearance from the female of this species.

Adult male Mexican Blonde emerging from its old skin. Note the contrast in appearance prior to its final molt.

This female Thailand Black has just emerged from its old skin.

This *Lasiodora parahybana* is emerging from its old skin while lying on its side.

molt and will usually die within a year. Mated females can store the sperm from several months to over a year before laying eggs. If they molt before the eggs are laid, they will shed the sperm along with their exoskeleton.

I usually try to preserve the freshly molted skin and reshape it so that when it dries, it appears to be a real tarantula. If you find the exuviae shortly after it has been shed, it can easily be reshaped. If it is already hard and brittle, try soaking it in hot water for a few minutes before shaping and drying it to look like the original.

Poecilotheria regalis, commonly called the Indian Ornamental.

Notes on Tarantulas in Nature

I was very fortunate to be the recipient of a Lilly Endowment Grant in 1990 and was able to spend the summer studying the behavior of tarantulas in nature. I made three separate trips to the southwestern United States during the months of June, July and August. A count was taken of the burrows at each location of the study. If there were less than five within a half acre area, then none were removed, but more than 85 percent of the tarantulas were left within their natural surroundings in any event. I also took a variety of species of different ages to leave a more natural

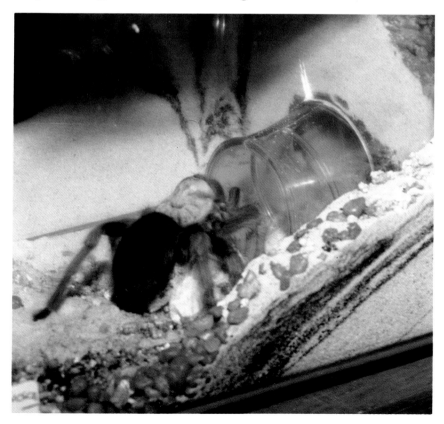

This Mexican Blonde is closing the egg sac she has just filled.

balance. Some locations contained only one or two burrows, while other areas held over 30 burrows. The local population is probably based on the abundance of the food supply in the area. Often at dusk or in the early morning hours, male tarantulas could be seen roaming across the highways and through the desert.

My two sons, Ben and John, accompanied me on the outing. In June, we had little luck locating tarantula burrows. We saw no adult males on the highways in Oklahoma or Texas and did not even find burrows until we reached Tucson. There, we located seven adults in burrows in an old lot across from an apartment complex. They were all light brown, almost blonde, and I assumed they were adult females. We selected out two and returned to the motel with them. Within two hours, one had turned on its back to molt. It turned out to be an adult male, and upon molting, was very black with a copper carapace. I quickly realized that the males and females of this particular species (Mexican Blonde) did not resemble one another (as the Mexican Red Leg or Pink Toe Tarantulas do).

After talking with several arachnologists, I learned that the local males usually molt into maturity in late June through to August. After their final molt, they leave their burrows and roam until their deaths in search of females. During the day, they usually protect themselves from heat and predators by staying under rocks or other refuges, and most begin their journey in search of a mate at night. However, some activity may be seen on overcast days, early mornings and late afternoons. The males can continue to mate with different females until they finally succumb.

Our July trip was the most productive. We found burrows in locations where they had not been during the first trip. The males were out roaming everywhere at night. I interviewed many local residents and learned that, in their opinion, this was a very unproductive tarantula year. Usually after the rains come in early July, these tarantulas can be seen on the roads. Some years seem more plentiful than others.

Holes appeared to be everywhere in the desert. We found several other arachnids, such as solpugids, vinegaroons, and scorpions, everywhere. We learned to recognize the difference in these types of burrows and those of a wolf spider's burrow compared to those of a tarantula. My sons became quite skillful at locating tarantula burrows.

The best method I found for safely securing a

As a pair of Mombassa Golden Starburst Tarantulas begin courtship, the male approaches from the top by tapping his front legs on the sides of the tank.

tarantula from a burrow was to flood it out. I carefully inserted a screwdriver at about a 45-degree angle from the ground until it was just ready to break through the burrow wall at about three inches beneath the surface. Next, I poured a gallon of water into the entrance. The second the tarantula rose to the surface, I inserted the screwdriver through the burrow wall, preventing the tarantula from retreating back down into the hole. After the initial examination, if we did not wish to remove it, we simply photographed it and let it return to its home. If we needed to capture it, I angled the screwdriver to push it up and out of the burrow opening without causing any harm to the tarantula. If the tarantula did not immediately appear, we did not continue to pour water, instead assuming the burrow was abandoned or had young at the bottom.

Two other methods were used that were not as successful as flooding. One way was to tease the tarantula out using a weed and wiggling and tapping it at the entrance. The tarantula sometimes mistook it for an insect and tried to capture it, but we had to be quick in order to catch the tarantula. The minute it spotted something towering above its burrow, or it realized there was no bug, it would dart back down the hole and would not climb back up under any circumstances. Only one tarantula and two solifugids were captured using this method.

We also tried digging the tarantula out, but not only could this injure the animal, it could make an awfully big hole in the ground. Digging can be instructive in that you can learn a lot about the structure of the burrow. We almost always found that the burrows would go straight down about five inches and then angle to one side. Many of the tarantula galleys were connected to abandoned rodent burrows and had many branches that the tarantula could use to protect and conceal itself. On two occasions, the burrow branched into three or four different directions and was about five feet long and two feet deep.

Tarantula burrows were found both in remote and in populated areas. The burrow hole was always flat against

A burrow of a Mexican Blonde found in Douglas, Arizona. At night, the tarantula will position itself near the entrance and wait for unsus-pecting insects to walk past the burrow.

the ground without a lip around it like certain burrowing wolf spider species build. Tarantulas may build the burrow out in the open as spiderlings and later, grasses begin to encroach near the hole. The tarantula tries to keep the area clear of debris around the hole so that insects have easy access. The very tiny tarantulas enlarge their burrows each year as they grow. If the home is destroyed, the tarantula may take up residence in an abandoned rodent burrow or under a rock. As an adult, it will not build a new hole from scratch, but it may enlarge an already existing hole.

We learned from our July field trip that burrows are occasionally destroyed by flash flooding, which is not uncommon in the southwestern United States. While visiting a canyon near Douglas, Arizona, a flash flood overtook us after we had located and marked over 20 burrows with sticks.

The rain was intense and within five minutes, flood waters were surging across the canyon. Within minutes, inches of water covered the ground and all our containers were floating. We were going to stay and see if the tarantulas came out of the holes, but we noticed that the dirt road our car was parked on was caving in and the car was leaning to one side. We quickly grabbed the containers and ran to the car. On the way, my son saw a tiny tarantula clinging to a blade of grass and he snagged it on the first try. It turned out to be the tiniest tarantula that we found and Ben named it Spud. Upon returning to this area on our next trip, we could only locate six tarantula burrows; the rest had been sealed off by the mud.

On the final trip in August, we saw few tarantulas. We still found over 20, but most of the burrows were sealed shut with mud. Since we had marked tarantula burrows previously, we were able to see how the tarantula covers its burrow entrance with mud and debris. The tarantula will seal the burrow during the winter and remove the soil and debris when it is ready to begin feeding in spring. It may often seal the burrow up again in June prior to molting. This is probably the reason I could not locate any burrows in Texas and New Mexico on my trip in June. Perhaps the tarantulas sealed the burrows in August because they had mated and wanted to deter other males from trying to mate with them again. Another hypothesis may be that since it was extremely hot in August, if they had fed well, they might have been waiting for the weather to cool down in September to open them again. At first, I thought they had young in the burrows in August, but I later learned that they mate in the summer and lay eggs the following spring, with the spiderlings hatching around June. Perhaps the burrows were sealed in June, not only for molting, but also because the eggs had hatched. Often the tarantula will not take food during the time it is protecting the egg sac.

Breeding Tarantulas

Breeding your tarantula is not necessarily a simple task. Even if you have successfully secured two of the same species, there is no guarantee that the female will be receptive to the male. Recently, I used a friend's male Mexican Red Leg in an attempt to mate it with five of my females. Only one female allowed the courtship and it took two days of constant reintroduction of the male to coax her into the mood. It will be several months before the success of this mating is determined.

It is difficult to obtain both a male and female of the same species. Your chances of getting a compatible pair from a pet store are greatest with the South American Pink Toe, Chile Rose, or Haitian Black Tarantulas.

Male tarantulas cannot mate until they have developed their palpal bulbs or emboli, which occurs internally prior to their final molt. The easiest way to sex them is to look under the first pair of legs. If you see a little hook-like spur or conspicuous tuft of hair on these legs or small, dark shiny bulbs on the palps, it's male. The tibial spurs, if present, are used to secure the female's fangs during mating.

When mating, the male will first drum his palp on the ground and tap her with his front pair of legs. This seems to put her in a tranquil state so he can secure her fangs and raise the front of her body

Mexican Red Knees mating.

Chilean tarantulas (*Grammostola spatulata*) mating.

her, he has plenty of room to run away. However, on some occasions, the female will kill the male which benefits the female by supplying her with a large protein source for her developing eggs.

Obviously, in order to mate, the male tarantula must have strong front legs, spurs, and pedipalps that are not damaged. His spinnerets must also be in good working order. He needs these to make a sperm web—a thick layer of silk that he uses to place sperm from his abdomen before drawing it up into the palpal bulbs by means of capillary action. Sometimes, the male will make a new sperm bed after mating with a female or may produce and destroy several of them before mating.

There is another way to distinguish a male from a female, but it requires a great deal of study and practice. After the tarantula has molted five or six times, many of them can be sexed using the skins. This can be a difficult and frustrating process. I have been practicing it for over two years now and have been successful most of the time. At the epigastric furrow

upward. He will then stroke her abdomen with his palps before inserting the embolus tip from his palpal bulb into her epigynum. Most males will use both their palpal bulbs, one after the other. Once his sperm has been deposited, he slowly lowers the female down and backs quickly away.

Most male tarantulas are not harmed by the female. In nature, the burrows are usually in an open area, so once the male mates with

opening on the inside of the abdominal skin, the female will have a hard lip-shaped horizontal structure that will not be present on males or immature females. A powerful magnifier or

delicate, multi-layered egg sac which will house the young spiderlings. Both sexes can get along minus a leg or two, but they cannot successfully produce a sperm web or an egg sac

Note the contrast in the male (left) and the female Thailand Black as they prepare to mate. In this particular species, there is a higher fatality rate for the males following the mating.

microscope is needed to detect it, but with practice, this method can be very rewarding, and if you wish to raise tarantulas, it could prove very useful to know males and immature females from females.

Males and even more importantly, females, must have undamaged spinnerets. She needs them to make the

without their spinnerets.

Often, pet store owners will tell me that a tarantula is male or female based on its color or the length of its legs. These are not accurate identification techniques to use with tarantulas. It is usually true that mature males have a much longer leg span than their female counterparts, but this

The male Mexican Red Knee on the left is seen raising the female into position for mating.

occurs after they reach full maturity. At times, males may have narrower abdomens than females even before they reach maturity; however, many females also have narrow abdomens. If the tarantula has just been taken from its natural environment, it will be likely to have a narrow abdomen. The tarantula owners are probably the ones who give them their plump abdomens from feeding them so much. In deserts in the southwestern United States, I found no females that were

plump except ones that were already carrying eggs. After a summer of hearty feeding the females fatten up, but in the spring they all have abdomens of about the same size. If you put two tarantulas side by side, it may be easier to distinguish which is male, but I would not depend upon this method to make accurate predictions. The best way to sex your tarantula when it is not yet mature is to examine its discarded abdominal exoskeleton.

Upon returning from the

field trip in August, I began pairing my tarantulas, attempting through trial and error to mate them. A male and female considered compatible would be placed together in a large box. Sometimes, the male would begin vibrating and tapping his palps and the female would respond immediately. Other times, he would try to court her and she would retreat. If he became irritated, he would run quickly over the side of the box.

Using this method, 11 pairs of the tarantulas collected on my field trip were successfully mated. Also mated was a previously acquired pair of Mombassa Golden Starburst Tarantulas.

I had high hopes that some tarantulas caught in August had already been mated, noticing during copulation that the males used both their palps. Usually, the tarantulas would insert the embolus of their left pedipalp and then the right. Some courtships lasted only a few seconds, while others lasted three or four minutes. (The courtship of my Mombassa Tarantulas lasts about 25 minutes.)

After the tarantulas were mated, they were fed and placed in larger containers for the winter. In April, they were offered food for the first time in three months and they fed readily.

On April 13, a female was noticed laying down a thick silken sheet covering an area of about six-by-six inches. I had not mated this particular tarantula; she was a large one that had remained in my home all winter. She laid her eggs and covered most of them with silk, but by morning she had begun devouring them. Tarantulas will sometimes do this if the eggs are not fertile or if they are startled or sense danger. The remaining dozen or so eggs were removed, rewrapped, and placed in an incubator in an attempt to hatch them. They dried and blackened within a week.

The next day, two more tarantulas had laid eggs. One had apparently mated in Arizona, but the other had mated in captivity. Both ultimately ate their young or eggs. A tarantula from South America that had mated the previous fall also laid eggs that same week with the same results. I had experienced this before as

my South American Pink Toe had also devoured her egg sac.

It is uncertain whether temperature, humidity, egg infertility, their captive status or a combination of these factors leads to this behavior. I hope to obtain more males and try each of these tarantulas again, and am certain of eventual success. Recently, my Mombassa Starburst Tarantula laid her egg sac and 75 spiderlings emerged healthy and plump.

The southwestern excursion taught me a great deal and that knowledge is used to make the most natural settings possible for tarantulas. The females' homes have been redesigned so that the probability of responding to a male that comes to call is as great as can be made in their natural environment. The burrows are built straight down for five inches and then across at an angle. The females sit at the top and grab insects as they wander by their burrows. They even wait until evening to go to the entrance. With each new idea, I am finding more success with my breeding program. I have videotaped the females drumming down inside their burrows in response to the palpal tapping from the male on the surface of the tank. In the spring, I hope these females will be producing egg sacs.

Raising Young Tarantulas

Many of my tarantulas have laid eggs and produced spiderlings. I also have a lot of experience in caring for very young spiderlings obtained from other collectors. I have raised several hundred tarantulas to maturity from the egg case. I have even hand-fed several Pink Toe spiderlings.

If you are fortunate enough to suddenly acquire hundreds of spiders when they first leave the egg sac, you are faced with a difficult task. In nature, the spiderlings cannibalize one another. It can be very difficult to find tiny insects to feed all the young. I suggest that you allow them to feed on one another for a few days. I recently separated 318 Texas Brown spiderlings from their egg sac collected from the southern Texas coast. Since the mother rejected caring for the egg sac after she arrived, I had to predict the

A silken menagerie created by a Mombassa Golden Starburst. She is visible on the bottom left. This menagerie will help to protect the young.

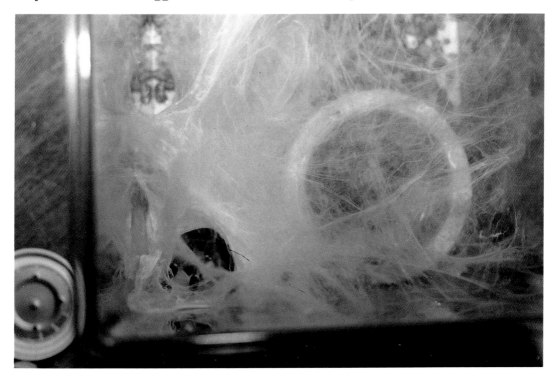

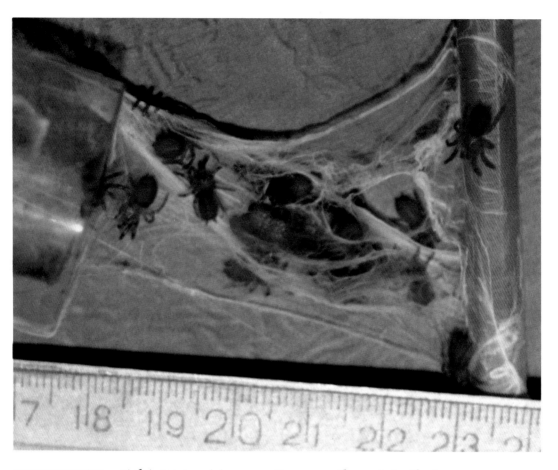

These spiderlings of the Mombassa Golden Starburst are only three days old.

right moment to open it. There are currently over 250 of those spiderlings still being cared for. They are fed with tiny fruit flies from a colony culture. If this is not readily available to you, then the young tarantulas may feed on the juices of a split-open cricket. If this proves successful, continue to use the method for a few weeks. Once they are feeding and strong, you can separate them into their own cages, but it is best not to do this until you can obtain a constant supply of food for them. Some pet stores sell baby crickets, but most of them are still too large for a young tarantula. If you want to try to raise crickets on your own, they would be ideal for the baby tarantulas. All crickets really need to reproduce is a moist sponge or sand, in which they lay their eggs.

When the spiderlings reach about two months of age, you can begin to feed them by hand. The ones living on the floor of the tank are not a problem since they will capture food on their own. They can capture and devour a cricket the same size as themselves, and this

Pink Toe, must be hand fed. They can usually capture a cricket slipped into the opening of their web enclosure. The assistance is needed because the baby cricket cannot climb up to the web.

Make sure you use an extremely small and shallow water dish for the

Mexican Red Knee protecting her egg sac.

is really an amazing event to observe. Sometimes, the tarantula may be turned upside down and it will continue to hold onto the cricket. The tarantulas that cling to the side of the tank in small web enclosures, such as the South American

spiderlings. A moist sponge or cotton ball is the preferred method. The spiderling can obtain the moisture it needs and there is less danger of it drowning in the dish of water. Small medicine bottle lids can be used for older spiderlings.

There are many species that mate and lay eggs year round. Generally, American species mate in the late summer to fall, and eggs are laid and hatch in the spring (with about 300–600 or more eggs). In extreme southern Texas, mating in the field occurs as early as May.

Although tarantulas lay great numbers of eggs, only a small number will reach full adulthood in nature. There are too many predators in the wild that feed on the young spiderlings before they can make their own burrows. The arboreal species lay fewer eggs and their spiderlings are larger when they hatch. I have found them much easier to care for than the burrowing species.

It's exciting to raise the tarantula yourself from a small spiderling. You get to experience the change in coloration as well as observe its rate of growth. Plus, you will have a pet that will be with you for a very long time.

Benefits to Man

There are far too many people in this world that do not realize the tremendous benefit that spiders provide for us. When I present my tarantula demonstrations, I often hear that the first thing someone would do when they spotted a spider is to step on it. I shudder every time I think about it. Spiders are very important to us. They are probably responsible for controlling more insects than any other order of arthropods. If it were not for spiders, we quite possibly would be overrun by insects. Of course, if that were to happen, then the insects might consume all our plants and trees. Without the vegetation, man would also die.

Another common complaint of people is in regard to the spiders occupying their home. The spiders would not be in the house if there was not a food supply readily available, at least, not for long. Sometimes, a large wolf spider may venture in by mistake, but I am not referring to these interesting specimens. The small house spiders that thrive in the house are living off tiny insects and mites. It is probably best to let the spiders rid your house of these pests.

Spider silk and venom have also proven beneficial to man. The silk is very strong and has been used in gunsights, microscopes and lenses. The venom is providing drugs used in the treatment of strokes, seizures, and other neurological disorders. The chemicals present in the venom prevent brain damage people may suffer as a result of these ailments.

Adult male Mombassa Golden Starburst.

This Mexican Blonde has briefly emerged from her artifical burrow opening.

Scientists have patterned a family of chemicals, called arylamines, after those found in spider venom.

Since there are only a few genera that can really cause man any harm, and they seldom come in contact with man, I feel that we should give these creatures the respect they deserve. They provide us with countless benefits and offer us opportunities to appreciate their intriguing lives. Having tarantulas as pets has given me a great opportunity to enjoy these fascinating animals. If more people could learn to respect instead of fear these animals, then I know we would all benefit from the experience.

Very Common Tarantula Questions

Question 1. Why does my tarantula often sit on the sponge in its water dish?

The tarantula may need more humidity or may be too warm. Do not be overly concerned. Keep the water dish full of water. In nature, condensation forms in their burrows at night, helping them with their humidity requirements. It may be wise to occasionally mist part of the tank if your tarantula spends too much time on its water dish. Remove anything that starts to mold as this can be harmful to the spider.

Question 2. Why does my tarantula sit curled up in a corner of its tank or sometimes stand high on its toes?

It may be too cold. Tarantulas require temperatures of around 75 degrees or so Fahrenheit. If the temperature stays below 65 degrees for too long, it will stop eating and may begin overwintering habits. If it becomes extremely cold, it may become ill as it slows down and stops eating and drinking.

Question 3. Why does my tarantula sit in the middle of the tank with its legs drawn in and partially under its body?

Your tarantula may be dying. It may be an older one that has already lived a full life. Sometimes, the tarantula is severely dehydrated or may have a disease or internal parasite. Try putting it on shallow water in a little dish.

Question 4. If a tarantula bites me, will it hurt?

A tarantula bite is similar to a bee sting, only more like two bees stinging at once. A small red mark or bump may occur, but it is essentially harmless. Only individuals who experience an allergic reaction to bee or other insect or spider bites need to be concerned. However, there is often no advance warning of whether or not a particular person may have allergies. There have been reports of patients being hospitalized for pain and swelling. Since there is so little known about the effects of

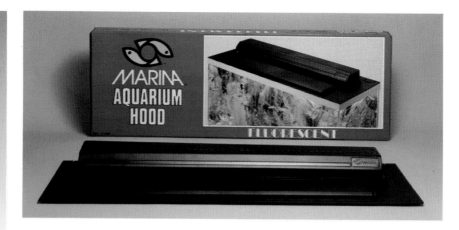

tarantula venom on humans, it is best to exercise caution when handling your tarantula. Therefore, the less aggressive species are recommended for the amateur fancier.

Question 5. Why do some tarantulas quickly rub their abdomens with their back legs when something moves near it?

This is the tarantula's defense against its vertebrate enemies like certain mammals or birds. It is kicking or flicking urticating hairs from its abdomen toward the intruder. These hairs act like little barbs that penetrate the attacker's skin in an attempt to get it to break off the attack. They may affect you with varying degrees of itching if they get on your hands or body. A tarantula that is accustomed to being handled will not usually throw these hairs at its owner.

Question 6. Does my tarantula need a place to hide?

In the wild, tarantulas conceal themselves in burrows either above or below ground, depending on the species. It is probably best to provide a hiding place for them in your terrarium. It is easy to select something to satisfy them, while, at the same time, allowing you to view them in their hiding place. Placing two rocks several inches apart with a flat rock on top provides you with a simple retreat for your pet. For arboreal species, use an angled piece of branch or bark.

Question 7. What size container should I use for its home?

Large aquariums are nice, but you don't need to overdo it. The cage should be at least twice the length of its body and twice as wide as its width. The height should not be greater than twice the length of its leg span. Tarantulas like to climb, but a fall from a long distance could kill them. The exoskeleton of their abdomen is a thin, membrane–like tissue that will easily split if dropped.

Question 8. What if my tarantula becomes injured?

Tarantulas have a slow metabolism. If it becomes injured and you can visibly see fluid escaping from the body, then there is little you can do. It will usually take it several days to die from a minor injury, or several days to heal. Alum powder mixed with water to form a paste can be applied to stop the bleeding after minor injuries. This method has been successful several times and the tarantulas have survived. It does not work for a severe injury or major trauma.

Question 9. What if my tarantula is missing a leg or a pedipalp, or loses one in a fall?

When a tarantula molts, the leg or palp will be replaced. It may not always be as big or colored the same as the other legs, but an additional molt should bring it back to the same size and color as the original. Legs, pedipalps, spinnerets and even chelicerae can be regenerated in this manner.

Question 10. How do I know when my tarantula is getting ready to bite?

Some tarantulas are very quick and you will have no warning. However, most will raise their front legs and pedipalps in a typical

A few nice plastic plants will improve the appearance of your terrarium. Photo courtesy of Hagen.

warning posture. Their fangs will also open and protrude outward. Some species will suddenly tap the intruder with their front legs as a type of warning.

Question 11. How do you tell a male from a female?

Except for the mature male, it is difficult to tell them apart. Upon reaching maturity, the males' pedipalps are enlarged with bulbs and mating spurs are generally present under the front pair of legs on most species. Experts can tell sometimes by examining the discarded abdominal exoskeletons of mature spiders, but it requires a lot of training and experience to successfully sex the spiders. Often, people say you can tell the differences by the length or shape of their legs, their color, or their size, but these methods have not proven entirely reliable.

Question 12. Can two tarantulas share the same cage?

No, they cannot stay together in the same cage. You may be able to get away with it for a short period of time if both are well fed, but remember that tarantulas are solitary, cannibalistic

predators and will fight and kill one another if given the opportunity. With tarantulas, as with most arthropods, there are exceptions. Some tropical tarantulas are communal, or social, to a degree.

Question 13. What kind of tarantula makes the best pet?

In general, most North American tarantulas like the Texas Brown and the Mexican Blonde are very gentle. The South American Pink Toe and the Mexican Red Leg are usually good natured. The Costa Rican Zebra and the Chile Rose also make good pets. Do not buy a tarantula that readily shows aggression or often displays an attack position.

Question 14. Where do tarantulas live in the wild?

Tarantulas live in warm climates all over the world between the 45° latitudes, except in Tasmania, New Zealand, the Hawaiian Islands and the South Pacific Islands. Most of them burrow into the ground, but others live on the sides of embankments, in tree cavities or among bromeliads.

Where to Find the People, Resources and Books to Answer The Questions

TARANTULA AND GENERAL SPIDER PUBLICATIONS

Austin, A. D. & N. W. Heather. *Australian Arachnology.* The Australian Entomological Society, Brisbane, 1988.

Baerg, W. J. *The Tarantula.* University of Kansas Press, Lawrence, 1958.

Breene, R. G., D. A. Dean, M. Nyffeler & G. B. Edwards. *Biology, Predation Ecology and Significance of Spiders in Texas Cotton Ecosystems with a Key to the Species.* Texas Agric. Exp. Stn. Bull. (In Press), 1992.

Browning, J. G. *Tarantulas.* T.F.H. Publications, Inc., New Jersey, 1989.

Foelix, R. F. *The Biology of Spiders.* Harvard University Press, Cambridge, London. 306 pp., 1982.

Kaston, B.J. *How to Know the Spiders.* Wm. C. Brown Company Publishers, Iowa, 1979.

LaBonte, G. *The Tarantula.* Dillion Press, Inc. Minneapolis, 1991.

Levi, H. W. & L. R. Levi. *Spiders and their Kin.* Golden Press, New York, 1990.

Preston-Mafham, R. & K. Preston-Mafham. *Spiders of the World.* Facts on file publishing, New York, 1984.

Preston-Mafham, R. *Spiders, an Illustrated Guide.* New Burlington Books, London, 1991.

Schultz, S. A. *The Tarantula Keeper's Guide.* Sterling Publishing Co. Inc., New York, 1984.

Smith, A. M. *The Tarantula, Classification and Identification Guide.* Fitzgerald Publishing, London, 1986.

Smith, A. M. *A Revision of the Theraphosidae Family from Africa and the Middle East.* Fitzgerald Publishing, London, 1991.

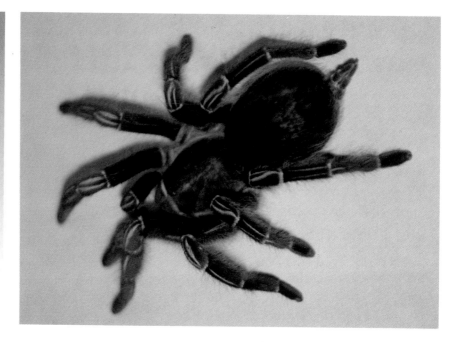

Costa Rican Zebra.

INDIVIDUALS

James W. Berry, Ph.D. Department of Biological Sciences, Butler University, Indianapolis, Indiana 46229 USA.

Robert Gale Breene III, Ph.D., Editor, The American Tarantula Society, P.O. Box 3594, South Padre Island, Texas 78597 USA.

Jonathan A. Coddington, Ph.D., National Museum of Natural History, Washington, DC 20540 USA.

Peter Kirk, Editor, British Tarantula Society, 21 Merganser Gardens, Thamesmead West, London SE28 ODH ENGLAND.

Ann Moreton, The Spider Museum, Route 2, Box 114, Powhatan, Virginia 23139 USA.

Steve Skinner, Vice-President, American Tarantula Society, 17336 Harper 02, Detroit, Michigan 48224-1963 USA.

Louis Sorkin, Ph.D., American Museum of Natural History, New York City, NY 11503 USA.

Rick C. West, Royal British Columbia Museum, c/o 4034 Glanford Avenue, Victoria, B.C. V8Z3Z6 CANADA

English Names, Scientific Names, and Habitats for Some Common Tarantulas

BOLIVIAN STEELY BLUE LEGGED
Pamphobeteus antinous
Rain forest

BURST BABOON (PAMPAS TAWNY RED, BRAZIL)
Grammostola pulchripes
Scrub and savannah

CAMPINA GRANDE SALMON PINK
Lasiodora parahybana
Rain forest

CHILE ROSE (OR BEAUTIFUL)
Grammostola cala
Shallow burrows, Mediterranean-type shrub vegetation

CHILE ROSE (OR COMMON)
Grammostola spatulata
Grammostola pulchripes
Shallow burrows, Mediterranean-type shrub vegetation

CHILEAN YELLOW RUMP
Paraphysa manicata
Mountain scrubland

COBALT BLUE (BURMA/ THAILAND)
Haplopelma (Melopoeus) lividus
Tropical wet forest

COLOMBIAN GIANT BIRD EATERS
Acanthoscurria sp.
Rain forest

COLOMBIAN PURPLE BLOOM
Pamphobeteus insignis
Pamphobeteus fortis
Rain forest

COSTA RICAN BLUE FRONT
Citharacanthus crinirufus
Tropical dry forest

COSTA RICAN RED LEG
Megaphobema mesomelas
Rain forest

COSTA RICAN SUN TIGER
Crypsidromus zebrata
Tropical wet forest

COSTA RICAN ZEBRA
Aphonopelma seemanni
Tropical dry forest

EAST AFRICAN HORNED BABOON
Ceratogyrus bechaunieus
Dry scrub and savannah

ENTRE RIOS (BRAZIL)
Grammostola iheringi
Mixed woodland

FEATHER FOOTED BABOON
Stromatopelma grisepes
Tropical forest

GOLIATH BIRD EATER (BRAZIL)
  Theraphosa blondi
  Rain forest
HAITIAN BLACK
  Phormictopus cancerides
  Tropical wet forest
HONDURAS/COSTA RICA BROWN
  Euathlus albopilosa
  Tropical wet forest
INDIAN ORNAMENTAL
  Poecilotheria regalis
  Deciduous dry forest
KING BABOON
  Citharischius crawshayi
  Desert and scrub
MEXICAN BLONDE
  Aphonopelma chalcodes
  Desert and scrub
MEXICAN RED KNEE
  Brachypelma smithi
  Tropical dry forest and scrub
MEXICAN BLACK VELVET
  Brachypelma vagans
  Tropical dry forest and scrub
MEXICAN TRUE RED LEG
  Brachypelma emilia
  Tropical dry forest and scrub
MOMBASSA GOLDEN STARBURST
  Pterinochilus murinus
  Scrub
SINGAPORE REDDISH BROWN
  Coremiocnemis validus
  Rain forest
SOUTH AMERICAN HORNED
  Sphaerobothria

hoffmanni
  Wet deciduous forest
SOUTH AMERICAN PINK TOE
  Avicularia avicularia
  Silk tubes, folded leaves, tropical wet forest, and rain forest
SOUTH AMERICAN TIGER RUMP
  Avicularia pulchra
  Silk tubes, folded leaves, tropical wet forest, and rain forest
SOUTH AMERICAN YELLOW
  Avicularia sp.
  Silk tubes, folded leaves, tropical wet forest, and rain forest
TEXAS BIG BEND GOLD
  Aphonopelma heterops
  Scrub
TEXAS BROWN
  Aphonopelma hentzi
  Scrub
THAILAND BLACK OR EDIBLE
  Haplopelma (Melopoeus) minax
  Tropical wet forest
TRINIDAD CHEVRON
  Psalmopoeus cambridgei
  Tropical wet forest
TRINIDAD MAHOGANY BROWN
  Tapenauchenius plumipes
  Silk tubes and folded leaves
WHITE COLLARED (URUGUAY)
  Pterinopelma saltator
  Pampas plain

Suggested Reading

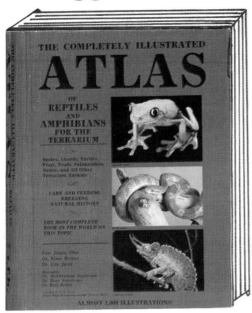

T.F.H. offers the most comprehensive selection of books dealing with tarantulas. A selection of titles is presented below. These and many other works are available at your local pet shop.

H-1102, 830 pgs, Over 1500 photos, Hard Cover, 8¼ x 12¼ in.

TW-123, 256 pgs, Over 150 color photos, Hard cover, 5 x 7 in.

PS-749, 96 pgs, Soft cover, 5½ x 8 in.

KW-075, 128 pgs, Hard cover, 5½ x 8 in.

CO-024S, 96 pgs, Over 80 color photos Soft cover, 5½ x 8½ in.

RE-124, 64 pgs, Over 50 color photos Soft cover, 7 x 10 in.

INDEX

Page numbers in boldface **refer to illustrations.**

Ambushers, 4
Anal tubercle, **11**
Aphonopelma anax, **52**
Aphonopelma chalcodes, **4**, **10**, **33**, **37–38**, **54**
Aphonopelma seemanni, **16**, **60**
Apodeme, **11**
Arachnida class, 5–6
Arboreal species, 5–6, 15, 23, 27, 30, 52, 56
Avicularia avicularia, 6, **15**, **18**, **29**
Bites, 5, 12–13, 15, 17, 20, 55
Bot flies, 22
Brachypelma emilia, **14**
Brachypelma smithi, **4**, **43**, **46**, **51**
Carapace, 9, 31, 38
Cephalothorax, 7, 9, **11**, 15, 25
Chericerae, 4, 8–9, **11**, 57
Chilean tarantula, 6
David, Al, 21–22, 30
Edigastric furrow, **11**, 44–45
Egg sac, 49
Embolus, 8, 43–44, 47
Epigynum, 44
Eucratoscelus longiceps, **8**
Exoskeleton, 6, 21, 29–32, 35, 57–58
Exuviae, 31, 35
Eyes, 9, **11**
Fangs, **11**, 13–14, 20, 31–32, 43, 58
Fovea, 11
Fruit flies, 50
Grammostola cala, **17**
Grammostola spatulata, **44**
Ground dwelling species, 6, 23
Handling, 18, 29, 55
Haplopelma lividus, **9**
Haplopelma minax, **12–13**, **34**, **45**
Health, 17–18
Hemolymph, 22
Hemolymph pressure, 31
Humidity, 24, 28, 48, 55
Hunters, 4

Injuries, 21–22, 57
Insecticides, 20
June beetles, 26
Lasiodora parahybana, **31**, **35**
Lasiodora species, **22**
Life span, 5–6
Lung slits, **11**
Maintenance, 23
Mating spurs, 6, 32, 58
Metabolism, 57
Mite infestations, 21, 24
Pamphobetus species, **7**
Papal bulb, 43–44
Pedicel, 7, **11**
Pedipalps, 6–8, **11**, 32, 44, 47, 57–58
Pepsis wasp, 20
Phormictopus cancerides, **48**
Poecilotheria regalis, **36**
Psalmopoeus cambridgei, **9**, **24**, **26**
Pterinochilus murinus, **23**, **39**, **49**, **50**, **53**
Scorpions, 6, 39
Silk, 4, 9–10, 30, 44, 53
Solifugids, 6, 40
Solpugids, 39
Spiderlings, 23, 45, 49–52, **50**
Spinnerets, 9–10, **11**, 44–45, 57
Temperature, 28, 48, 55
Terrariums, 16, 23–25, 51, 56,
Theraphosa blondi, **25**, **27**
Theraphosidae family, 5, 9
Threatened Species List, 14
Ticks, 6
Trappers, 4
Urticating hairs, 9, 17, 19, 56
Venom, 5, 20, 53–56
Vermiculite, 24
Vinegaroons, 39
Wandering Spiders, 4
Water, 16, 24–25, 28–29, 31–32, 51, 55
Web Builders, 4
Whipscorpions, 6
Wolf spider, 39–40, 53

Inside front cover photo by Michael Gilroy; inside back cover photo by Isabelle Francais.